KATSUGEN

The Gentle Art of Well-Being

By
Richard S. Omura

Katsugen – The Gentle Art of Well-Being
Copyright Richard S. Omura © 2000,
Revised Edition 2013 All Rights Reserved

Other books by Richard S. Omura:
The Seven Circles
The Tao of God
The Whole Universe Book
The Journey To The Center Of The Whole

http://www.RichardOmura.com

 (katsu) life

 (ghen) vigor, stamina, spirit, energy

DEDICATION

To Haruchika Noguchi and to my mother, Mariko Omura, who taught me that health is key to happiness.

TABLE OF CONTENTS

Foreword.....7

Preface: Katsugen Flow.....13

1. What is Katsugen?.....17

2. Starting Katsugen.....27

3. Chrysalis Emergence.....35

4. The Lifestyle and Philosophy.....46

5. The Purpose of Pain.....50

6. Physical Exercise.....55

7. Creativity.....61

8. Work, Stress and Relaxation.....65

9. Medical Science.....72

10. Mind and Spirit.....77

11. Pleasure.....85

12. Drugs.....89

13. Appearance.....92

14. Time and Faith.....96

15. Self-Mastery.....99

Afterword.....103

Life's difficulties come not from lack,
but from not using effectively what one has.

FOREWORD

The practice of which this book focuses upon is called *katsugen undoh* (ka'-tsu-ghen oon-doh) in Japan. *Katsugen* has a meaning close to "primal life energy" and *undoh* is simply defined as "exercise". I shortened it to *katsugen* because I wanted to make this book into something more than about just the exercise itself. It was my intent to relay my own personal experience of the katsugen life energy and how to tap into it, not only physically, but also mindally and spiritually.

I learned katsugen exercise from a healer named Haruchika Noguchi. My mother had taken me to him when I was a child suffering from medical problems. It goes back to Japan when I was in third grade going to a U.S. military dependents school at an army base. I was an "army brat." At Yoyogi Elementary School we would have periodic eye exams. At one of these my left peripheral vision on my left eye was found to be almost non-existent. It was, at first, attributed to what they called "lazy eye", a condition where one eye was weakened due to non-use. In an attempt to resolve this I was told to wear an eye patch over my right eye for a few weeks, to try to make my left eye work harder so that it would be strengthened from usage. This was not effective. Later on my head was x-rayed showing that I had a brain tumor behind my left temple causing my vision impairment.

Surgery was in the works. Being eight years old at the time, it was thought best for me not to be told of the impending operation. (A decision of which I am grateful. I would have been extremely frightened otherwise.) Because surgeons in Japan were very capable of this type of surgery and the alternative was to fly me to the U.S., I became an inpatient at Tokyo University Hospital.

I didn't know what was going on. I didn't feel sick and was not aware of any debilitating symptoms. My mother and grandmother told me I was there for a battery of physical exams. Nothing to worry about.

Then came the day of the "big exam". They shaved my head because they were going to "put a little pin in it," which, of course, would be completely painless, they said. I do remember, while being carted off into the elevator, that a nurse gave me an injection in my back that was excruciatingly painful. Then, I was wheeled into a large, well-lighted room with an assortment of shiny equipment and about a half dozen people dressed in green coveralls.

The last thing I remember in that room was lying on the bed and being told to slowly count to ten as I inhaled from a black rubber cup attached to a hose.

The operation was successful and I was out of the hospital in a week. Unfortunately, the tumor, which was about the size of a man's thumb, had done its damage. My pituitary gland was gone.

The pituitary gland is a small, oval endocrine gland that lies at the base of the brain. It is called the master gland because the other endocrine glands depend on its secretions for stimulation. The pituitary has two distinct lobes, anterior and posterior. The anterior lobe secretes at least six hormones: human growth hormone which stimulates overall body growth; ACTH (adrenocorticotropic hormone), which controls steroid hormone secretion by the adrenal cortex, thyrotropic hormone, which stimulates the activity of the thyroid gland; and three gonadotropic hormones, which control growth and reproductive activity of the gonads (ovaries in women, testes in men).

To put it in a nutshell, the loss of my pituitary gland meant that I couldn't grow and wouldn't have reproductive capabilities without help. Fortunately, medical science had made some inroads in this field. I was prescribed injections of human growth hormone once every two weeks and then testosterone shots once I became adolescent. Synthroid and prednisone were also part of my daily medicational regimen.

My mother had faith in medical science but she wanted to hedge her bets. Aside from having me see the doctors for my checkup and periodic tests following the surgery, she began taking me to a Japanese healer by the name of Harachiku Noguchi.

The memories of those days are hazy but I still remember the large Japanese mansion in which Noguchi-san maintained his practice. The house had big, black shingles on its roof (as do most Japanese houses) and was probably of pre-war construction and made entirely of wood. There was definitely a feeling of age about the abode. We took our shoes off when we entered (although taking shoes off is quite common in a Japanese domicile, nowadays it is not the case in most public places).

There were two main sections, both with *tatami* floors. Tatami is a thick plank woven out of straw about the size of a large western door. The tatamis were laid out and embedded side by side into the flooring.

One section was where people did their katsugen exercises and the other section was where Noguchi-san healed people. I think, originally, when it was a house used for regular living, that it consisted of two rooms and a hallway running alongside both rooms, but the paper sliding doors that used to separate the rooms and hallway were taken out and made into one large room. Those who waited to be treated sat on sofas or easy chairs that were lined up where the hallway used to be, that is, alongside the two sections. With the sliding doors taken out, the two sections were completely visible from the waiting area.

There was also a large, tan colored speaker box with a round speaker hole. From it came soothing classical music by which katsugen exercise was practiced. Was it Mozart? Haydn? Beethoven? I was too young and ignorant of classical music to know.

Noguchi-san was a kind, good-natured gentleman with longish graying hair dressed in a traditional Japanese brown *hakama* and charcoal gray kimono. He treated his patients sitting on a *zabuton* (small flat cushion). The order of treatment was like this: first you sat and waited on the sofas out front, then you were called in to the treatment section among about ten patients who also sat on zabutons about ten feet directly in front of Noguchi-san. As Noguchi-san finished treating his patient lying right before him, the next in line would get up and lie down to be treated.

There is much about Noguchi-san that I do not know. There are some Japanese books about the man but I believe only one has been translated into English. He was well versed in the healing arts and hopefully, more of his techniques will become known in the United States soon.

For now, suffice to say that his treatments helped me tremendously. The one thing from him that I can truly impart to others is the art of katsugen undoh. When he first taught it to me, I didn't quite understand it. I practiced it sporadically and not with much enthusiasm. It wasn't until I was an adult that I began to see its potentials.

Now that I am over the half-century mark (at the time of writing), I can see that katsugen exercise has made a remarkable difference in my life. I have had my problems when I was an adolescent, not only medical ones but psychological ones, stemming from my medical condition, which continue to a certain extent to this day. I had bouts with substance abuse. I was codependent of an alcoholic woman that I lived with for a number of years. My life surely had and still has its ups and downs but all through it all, I had the ability to tap into katsugen. Not just katsugen undoh, the exercise, but katsugen the primal life energy with its stamina, vigor and spirit. That is the reason why this book is called katsugen and not katsugen undoh. It is not only about katsugen exercise, but also about releasing this primal spirit energy within us into everyday use, to revive into your life the foundation of stability, peace, health and the source of boundless creative energy.

When the self reaches for the spirit
the intellect must step out of the way.

In like manner,

For the self to melt into the body,
the intellect cannot stay.

PREFACE: KATSUGEN FLOW

Your body and mind feel separate. Your mind wants to go up, your body wants to go down. There's a battle taking place inside you, two energies trying to dominate each other. The energy inside seethes, struggling to get out. You're a volcano with only limited ways to vent off your searing hot magma. If you don't find a path to channel your energy you'll explode...

So a time is set, a place of privacy designated, room to move allowed, and the appropriate music engaged. And you invoke KATSUGEN.

At first, your body feels like a rock, a statue, a mechanical robot...yet inside you know you're a living, breathing, feeling creature made of soft tissue, supple muscles and dynamic life plasm.

You want to break out of the robot shell, to burst the inhibiting bonds of the statue's mold. You're tired of acting in set ways, treading tired, old, familiar steps. You sense that your body was created to be moved in millions of free-form patterns, yet the constraints of society have shackled you, have chained you to a mere shadow of physical freedom. By invoking the flow, your body's natural creative energies will emerge, blooming like a flower.

As you become connected to the katsugen flow, the cares and concerns of the mundane world disappear. Your mind quits badgering your body. There is no PROPER way to be. PROPER becomes irrelevant. There is no PACE to keep. PACE is not of the now. Self-consciousness detaches itself from SHAME and INSECURITY. SHAME and INSECURITY are only illusions.

Bit by bit, the plaster falls from the statue. Plate by plate the robot's shell disassembles. Then, like the petals of a flower, your natural self unfolds.

The music leads you to move: your body yearns to sway. You sway. Your arms and hands want to move of their own accord. You let them. Your feet have a mind of their own. That's fine. YOUR BODY KNOWS. You let it be, keeping your mind on the music, not on your body.

The beat of the music urges you towards dance moves. But NO. You don't dance. Dance moves come from the mind and they only make you self-conscious of your appearance. The katsugen flow of your body is for your body, no one else. Not for observers. Not for your own mind. You let your body set the pattern. Your mind is detached. It does not tell your body anything. It does *not* say make little movements, make big movements, move happy, move sad. It says: *Be Free.*

The movement escalates. Your body moves in ways it never has before. Gravity is a help, not a hindrance. Floors and walls are supports, not obstacles. Like a child, you enjoy the movements of your body, swaying with the ethereal forces of your body's aura. Movement transcends thought, expressing exactly your relation to time and space. Time stands still. Space becomes tangible. You move in harmony with the All. There is peace in motion.

Peace, though, does not stay. There is a disturbance from within that wells up. You become aware of memories of the past few days which stressed your mind and body. These memories bring out impatience, anger, irritation, disgust, hate and other negative emotions and cause them to rise up to the fore; you can no longer keep them bottled up. Through the movements of your body you express them. Vibrations and shudders rack your body as it becomes extremely agitated by the release of those volatile energies. You keep letting it go, as those negative energies are expressed as movements of the various parts of your body. You wring your hands, shake your feet, twist your body, and jump up and down. You do whatever your body wants to do to let these pent up energies go.

As you release these energies, a great big desire to breathe overtakes you. You open your mouth. A huge *yawn* fills your face, a yawn such as you've never experienced before. It's as if you have finally awoken from a long sleep. Tears come into your eyes. Your nose runs. An awakening happens. It is as if your whole body is yawning, taking in the fresh new air of physical freedom released from the bonds of physical and emotional toxins.

You realize, at last, that your body is truly alive. Your body loves you.

The katsugen flow continues until your body is satisfied; then, the desire to move gives way to the desire to rest. And it is time to close the flow.

Your body once again becomes attached fully to your mind, yet now, the two seem to fit together more easily. There is more of a willingness on your body's part to become an integrated whole. It is easier now to shoulder the armor with which to face the rigors of living in this society.

For your mind loves your body and it will allow it freedom from time to time. In return, your body will love your mind. It will do as your mind bids, with little complaint, out of that love. Your mind will no longer find it necessary to have dictatorial domination over your body.

The battle between your body and mind has ceased.

You are one.

In circular motion
there is balance.
In and out, around and around,
Up, down, give and take.

Block this motion,
and the system comes to a halt.
Let it flow,
and it will fling off intruders
and keep on going.

WHAT IS KATSUGEN?

Katsugen is a way of letting the natural system of our bodies take care of itself; of maintaining and sustaining the circular balance of energy in our body.

It trains the natural system in all of us that keeps us healthy and unfettered by the arrogant attitude of the mind. This inner system includes the autonomic (involuntary) nervous system, which plays a major role in our health.

Dogs eat grass knowing somehow that it's good for their digestive system. Creatures throughout the animal kingdom instinctively know what vegetation to eat in order to feel better. How? They don't have medical knowledge, yet, they *know* because they're in tune with their body. Actually, they are *mostly* body. They don't have enough "mind" to *oppose* the body.

The body *knows* things that the mind doesn't.

Modern man, by putting the mind on a pedestal at the expense of the body, ignores the health urgings of what I will call the Innate Bodily Intelligence, or IBI

Your mind should not be in conflict with the IBI.

Rather, it should be in harmony, because basically, health is your body in harmony with its inner and outer environment.

In the present state of many people's thinking, the mind is thought of as separate from and superior to the body. This model of thinking creates conflict between the arrogance of our mind and our Innate Bodily Intelligence. Such conflict can result in otherwise avoidable illness, obesity, drug and other substance addictions, stress, and a host of mental and physical problems.

The purpose of katsugen is to allow the mind to throw off its illusions and increase its receptivity to the Innate Bodily Intelligence.

This will create harmony and unity in you so that you can function as a complete body/mind/soul unit – as an entity that is one and whole.

Katsugen is a movement that comes out of your Innate Bodily Intelligence. It is a way to exercise and tune up your autonomous (involuntary) nervous system. But it's not just exercise, or a dance, as most people would define dance.

Katsugen is appropriate for people of all ages, all physical abilities, even the physically challenged. It doesn't require faith (even though it helps) or any religious or spiritual affiliation, although I believe the IBI stems from a spiritual source.

Katsugen is a movement that is different for each person, each time that it is practiced. It is generally pleasurable and can last from just a few minutes to an indefinite length of time. It can be done alone or with a partner but it is more private than public. Make no mistake: It is not a cure-all. In fact, it is more a preventative measure than an instant fix. It is a lifestyle that will lead to fulfillment and well-being.

When disease or pain occurs, katsugen can ease you back in the right direction and can assist you in restoring your health. This may happen quickly, or it may take some time. It depends on your condition. Katsugen will not be able to set a broken bone or grow a new limb, but it will help you in healing and regaining your physical, emotional and psychological health.

It is often the times of transition that cause stress, pain and a falling out of health; such as when one starts or loses a job, gains or loses much weight, gains or loses a loved one, starts a new endeavor, or engages in anything that is not a routine event. During these transition times, katsugen will enable you to maintain a stable foundation of well-being, rooted in the balance of body, mind, and spirit.

It's possible that you have already experienced a mild form of katsugen. When people dance without being self-conscious, without thinking of steps, timing or how stupid or cool they look, they're pretty close to katsugen. Or when you just sit with your eyes closed, listening to music and swaying gently from side to side, completely oblivious to the outside world, you're letting the IBI have more control, so you are close to katsugen. But there's more to it than that. Quite a bit more.

There is your body. And there is your mind. (We'll leave out spirit for the purpose of this discussion.) Your body should do you well. It should provide you with the means of getting about for the purposes of work, play and pleasure. It's your tool. But like any complicated tool, you can't abuse it without it breaking down on you. It's like your car. Think of your mind as the driver and your body as the vehicle. You have to take the automobile's needs into consideration if you don't want to be left stranded on the freeway. You've got to change oil regularly, put the right kind of gas in, drive it carefully, and so on and so forth. You recognize the needs of the car by... how? By reading the manual. It's easy with your car, as it comes with a manual. Your body doesn't. Or does it? Read on.

A human manufacturer made your car. Nature/God made you. Now, a manual to a car has to be read, the manual for your body is accessed differently. It is automatically enabled.

It's what I've been calling the IBI, the Innate Bodily Intelligence. Maybe you're thinking, "But...how do you access your manual, the IBI?" You don't *read* the IBI, you *become* it. Remember the dog that ate the grass? Dogs can't read, but in this case it's to their benefit. They don't have a questioning mind asking itself, "What am I doing, eating this grass? I'm not a cow!" Their IBI says, "eat grass", and the dog does. Exactly like when you sneeze. Or cough. Or break wind.

The problem with us humans is that sometimes we're too intellectual for our own good and we often disable the IBI with our mind's preconceptions and misunderstandings.

The intellectual capacity of the mind is awesome. The human intellect is a tool that we should treasure and hone, but it is neither infallible nor more vital than the body or spirit. Unfortunately, our society has placed the mind's importance above our physical and spiritual endowments.

That's why we have nuclear weapons, environmental pollution and other disasters, which spring from intellectual thought that disregards bodily health and the spiritual origins and essence of each human being. In the case of our personal health, our own arrogant mind that we put on a pedestal is always countermanding our body's natural urges and demands.

So let me ask you this:

Is your body under the domination of your mind?

LIBERATE YOUR BODY!

> *"They who are the most effectively enslaved are they who are not aware of their chains."*

"What? My body isn't free?" you may ask. I don't know, is it? To find out, ask yourself these ten questions:

1. Do you frequently stifle your body's natural urges? Urges such as:
    a. belching, sneezing or coughing
    b. flatulence
    c. sex in any form
    d. eating and drinking
    e. yawning

f. yelling and screaming
   g. dozing off
   h. acting like a child
2. Do you work harder and longer than you want to? (Or do you work at all, when you don't want to?)
3. If you are a woman, do you keep your legs together when wearing a dress?
4. Do you exercise only in set patterns and with repetitious movements?
5. Are you self-conscious when you dance? (Or don't dance at all because you are too self-conscious?)
6. Are you disappointed in your athletic abilities?
7. Do you have an image in your mind of how you should act in order to be masculine (or feminine)?
8. Are you self-conscious about your weight?
9. Are you constantly regretting doing something that you feel you should not have done?
10. Do you get easily addicted to substances, (including caffeine, nicotine, alcohol and sugar)?

A 'yes' answer to any of these questions would mean, no, your body isn't free. It's under the domination of your mind.

Your mind is constantly ordering your body to behave in ways that it thinks is right and proper. I think it's one of the assumptions of civilization that your mind should maintain strict strait-laced control of the body.

Which is fine as long as the mind controls the body based on sound logic, reason and values. But what if the mind doesn't have the information right? For instance, a mind that believes a diet that's high in fat is good for the body can bring about heart disease by eating too much fatty food. A mind that thinks harmful drugs are healthy will abuse them and get addicted. When the mind is being fed information that is contradictory and confusing, its ability to control the body becomes dangerous. The mind is tricked by false information and can lead the body into habits that are detrimental for the entire body-mind system.

So, you think, "That's not true in my case. I know eating fatty food is not good for me, and likewise with drugs. My information is sound." Sure, but I wonder if that's always the case. Are the sources of your information that consistently reliable? I don't think so.

Isn't it common knowledge that people get their information from a lot of questionable sources? It starts during childhood. Parents usually have good intentions but tend to perpetuate and project their misconceptions and misunderstandings onto the next generation. Also, the social pressure put on you by your peers at school most likely influence how you act and think to this day.

And can you ignore the observation that your mind, and through it your body, are conditioned by television commercials, advertisements in magazines and on billboards, from movies and TV programs as well as by what other people say?

So, at first, your parents gave you their ideas on how you should behave, then teachers and fellow students influenced you with their standards of behavior. Now, the media bombards you with messages that soak into your subconscious level, telling you how you should look, dress and act in order to fit into what they want you to think is acceptable. No wonder so many people are confused!

Now, most of you know what I'm talking about. This is not new information. Of course, some of this conditioning blitz from family, friends and media *may* be necessary, useful and even valuable. But it is unfortunate that many people take this material and swallow it whole without questioning its validity. A lot of this stuff is *not* made up of concepts or values that you can put to the test by trying it out and seeing the results. These kinds of hype are composed of suggestions, images, association with accepted values, emotions, and other semi-subliminal techniques. The sad thing is that most people don't know how much they are being limited by them.

Even when you get your information from reliable sources such as your doctor or a health magazine, the material can be conflicting, and it very often becomes obsolete due to the influx of newly discovered information.

Now, don't get me wrong: I respect doctors and other health practitioners immensely, but they are not infallible. And they aren't *you*. *You* are the one that take the medicine and have to go through the medical procedures. *You* are the one that have to take the consequences of their information.

Katsugen is a way of evaluating this inflow of information by tuning up your IBI so that your body will instinctively know what works and what doesn't for you.

Here's another point: newly discovered facts about the human body are indispensable to maintaining your health. But how do you use those facts and effectively apply them to yourself?

For instance, medical science has proven convincingly that regular exercise and a careful diet is useful for controlling weight and decreasing the chance of heart disease.

This is wonderful. But what good is it if people can't get themselves to exercise regularly?

It's the same thing with diets. Everyone *knows* that you shouldn't eat food with too much sugar or fat. This bit of knowledge is also useless if your body *can't quit* craving those foods.

Your body is a wonderful, complex organism. Set it free and it will find the best path to follow. I'm including the brain (as opposed to the mind) as part of this physical organism. The unconscious part of your brain along with the involuntary nervous system operates the parts of your body that the conscious part does not.

For instance, you don't consciously tell your heart to keep on beating or your stomach to digest food. You don't have to. The components of your involuntary autonomic nervous system do it for you; they're like dedicated employees that are always working for you 24/7.

Your body also defends itself pretty well. When something gets stuck in your throat, you cough. When dust gets in your nose, you sneeze.

These are the self-defense mechanisms of the involuntary nervous system in your body that keep the undesirables out. Kind of like bouncers at a night club that you might own. If you keep telling your bouncers to lay off from time to time, they get lax. And next time you need them they might not be around. So it's good to keep them on their toes.

You'll find that once you start incorporating katsugen into your life, you'll have a cleaner complexion, a body that has an in-built knowledge of the most suitable foods for yourself, greater physical coordination, increased creativity, more desire to exercise, a healthy sense for finding your most easily maintained and best-suited weight, a sensitivity to balancing your life and an increased knowledge and awareness of how your body can most beautifully interface with your environment. All of these will increase your confidence, ability, poise, and improve your perspective in life.

Throughout the day, the human organism accumulates many physical and emotional toxins that, after time, could make us ill and die an early death. The physical toxins could come from food, water, air and other substances we consume. The emotional toxins usually come from unwanted circumstances and from unpleasant interactions with other people. Wherever and whatever they come from, they are detrimental to our well-being.

What if we could, at the end of each day, manage to delete all those toxins that we accumulated throughout that day so that we start out fresh the next morning? Maybe we would live forever. Or maybe not, but we would definitely be more healthy and live a longer life. This is the principle behind practicing katsugen every day. It would be virtually impossible to get rid of a hundred percent of the physical and emotional toxins we imbibe, but maybe we could do away with fifty percent, and even ten percent would be greatly beneficial to our physical and mental health. It is a natural process like respiration - breathing in and out. What you take in, you take out. It is a balancing of energies that happens naturally when the soul is freed from the constricting effects of human ego, intellect and hubris.

Keep in mind that katsugen goes hand in hand with a life style that is based on the premise that order and wisdom are inherent aspects of the body, mind and spirit; and of the universe. It is opposite and contrary to the school of thinking that believes in "no pain, no gain".

It is letting the natural beauty and creativity that we are all endowed with spring forth *without* physical, mental or spiritual stress.

For attaining things that are *not* already a part of us, hard, stressful work might be necessary. Katsugen is releasing something that has *already* been given us. Something that is *inside*, which due to our ignorance, we have stifled and repressed. It is not a striving, but a *relaxing*.

Not a grasping, but a *letting go*.

To learn katsugen, you must follow your instincts.

But actually, it is not something you learn. Rather, it's something that requires *unlearning* years of conditioning.

So, if your body is screaming to be unfettered from the restraints of society, raring to escape the years of being shackled and bound by propriety, twitching to be unleashed, delivered and set loose from the tyrant of your mind, the time is here. You can at last be free.

Relax.
Think about your body.
It's been a good friend;
it deserves some time of its own.

Release it from your mind's domination,
its insecurity, its sorrow and fear.
Once in tune with nature,
your body will know the best course to steer.

STARTING KATSUGEN

PREPARATION AND ENVIRONMENT

1. Space: Once learned, katsugen can start spontaneously, but unless you are in a location with lots of space and privacy, delay the urge until you have found or created the ideal place for it. Ideally, it's great to be able to use a large room but basically if you have enough room to swing your arms and to kick out your feet without hitting anything, that should be sufficient. You could, if necessary, practice katsugen in a tight area, but it would be as a last resort.

2. Privacy is also important. Turn off your phones and also make sure no one can walk in on you. You must feel safe and free from scrutiny and intrusion. This is especially important when you are just starting to get the hang of katsugen. Once you have a feel for it you can tailor the practice into your own personal lifestyle as you see fit. Katsugen in a group setting can stimulate the flowing of ki (chi/qi)

3. Music: katsugen can be stimulated and enhanced by music that moves you physically and emotionally. Katsugen can be done without music and sometimes I prefer it that

way. I use to use music more often than not, but now I don't use it as much. During katsugen my mind can use the music like a mantra so that its attention is drawn away from the body, while the body uses the music as a source of inspiration and expression. There is a drawback to using music when practicing katsugen and this is when you start to dance. Which is not altogether undesirable except when you start to want to "look good", to want to start doing dance moves derived from what your mind thinks looks "cool". When this happens, your mind slowly starts to dominate your body. But that's okay. Let it "get down" for a while. Then snap out of it and resume katsugen.

4. Position: The induction movements are usually done sitting down, but once you acquire the skill, it can be done standing up, or even skipped. After katsugen has been induced, it will carry you into various postures, positions and movements. When I am full of energy, my movements bring me up to my feet. When I am in need of relaxing, the movement will manifest in various reclined positions.

5. Meditation: If you know how to meditate, meditation can be helpful before or after practicing katsugen. Or, once you learn katsugen, practicing it before meditation can result in a deeper meditative state.

INDUCTION OF KATSUGEN

Sit in the middle of the room either on a stool or on your haunches, Japanese style. Sitting on the edge of a sofa is another option. It is important that you can relax without any pain or stress on any part of your body. If you are on a stool make sure it is not too tall; the soles of your feet must be flat on the floor and your knees bent. Sit upright with your back straight or with a slight arch. Rest the back of your hands on your lap. Close your eyes. Relax.

SPINE WARMUP: Casually twirl your shoulders around to one side, as if you were trying to look at the base of your spine. Go as far back as you comfortably can and then suddenly relax the tension and return to the forward facing position. Repeat this again in the other direction. Do this movement three to five times to the right, three to five times to the left. Relax.

(Although the accompanying photos show the movement being done to the left and then to the right, it does not matter which side you start from.)

INDUCTION MOVEMENT: Raise your arms up over your head, clench your fingers over your thumb and lower your elbows down while trying to bring your shoulder blades together. As you breathe out, tense this area between your shoulder blades for a second, and then release the tension suddenly as you breathe in. Lower hands to your lap and relax. Repeat this movement three to five times.

(This movement induces the autonomic nervous system to respond by doing something that is counter-intuitive to the body: Normally, a fist is made with the thumbs out, ki is projected forward and muscles are relaxed as you breathe out. The induction movement reverses this normal behavior and jolts the autonomic nervous system into acting.)

Now, just relax and sit quietly. The idea is to let your body move without your mind influencing its movements. Don't think about your body. Think about the music. Pick out a certain instrument or voice and casually focus your mind on it. Let your body be. And slowly, it will begin to want to move of its own accord. A gently swaying is what usually happens. A rotating of the neck or shoulders may also occur. Whatever movement you may be experiencing, just let it happen. Don't force the movement to become bigger or smaller, let the movement increase naturally. Don't become self-conscious about it.

Your mind should have at its focus, the point of ki (chi). Also known as the tanden (dantian), this point of ki is about two or three inches below your navel, located inside your body next to your spine. There is a big cluster of nerves there, the second largest such cluster in your body next to your brain. Lightly keep your mind on this point.

This cluster is often referred to as the second mind and is a source of great energy. Many martial arts disciplines as well as meditational practices use this point for focal concentration, as it is your body's center of gravity.

As you try to keep your mind on the tanden, your mind may wander to thinking about daily concerns or it may start to focus on the music, that is okay. Sometimes emotional memories will create a bigger movement, this is good. Express and release all your emotional tensions through your movements. Just go back to focusing on the point of ki when you remember.

You do not have to stay seated or remain in the same posture. When there is discomfort in the way you are positioned, your body will naturally want to change its posture. Don't hinder it. Let it move according to its own tendencies.

The movement may grow, or it may stay the same. It will feel good regardless of how vigorous or gentle the movement may become. Normally, the movement will get more animated. It may resemble dance at one point or another, but it should not be dance as is commonly known.

In katsugen, one moves using the ki point as the source of inspiration as opposed to using your brain as the source. In other words the movements come not a result of *thinking what to do* but as a result of *feeling what comes naturally*.

SPINE WARMUP (LEFT)

  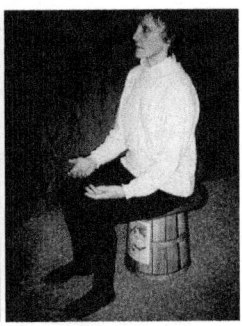

1. STARTING POSITION	2. TWIST	3. RETURN
Sit up straight with feet flat on the floor. Palms facing up. Eyes closed.	Gently look over your left shoulder toward the base of your spine. Hold position for one second.	Release all tension. Return to starting position. Repeat movements alternately three to five times each.

SPINE WARMUP (RIGHT)

INDUCTION MOVEMENT

1. STARTING POSITION

Sit up straight with feet flat on the floor. Palms facing up. Eyes closed.

2. LIFT ARMS

Make a fist with thumbs inside. As you slowly breathe in, raise arms slowly. Spread elbows back as you clench shoulder blades.

(continued next page)

3. TENSION

Now, breathe out as you put tension in the area between your shoulder blades. Increase tension for a few seconds, then suddenly relax, let go and breathe in.

4. RELEASE

After releasing tension return to first position.

Repeat movement three to five times.

Even love itself
must not be imprisoned
in one's own heart.
It must flow through you
so that it goes out to all.

So it is with every emotion.
It must flow in and out of you,
like the air you breathe.

It is easy to breathe "good" out,
when you breathe "good" in.
But how do you breathe "good" out
when you breathe "bad" in?

CHRYSALIS EMERGENCE

Many have experienced the beginning phase of katsugen. There are movement techniques that explore this early stage but they do not go beyond into the exercising of the involuntary nervous system. They do not completely emerge from the chrysalis and into katsugen. They stay within the cocoon of the mind-dominated body or at best the mind and body work in unison. Katsugen only happens when the mind frees the body so that the body takes precedence.

The emergence from the chrysalis comes when you actuate the urge to yawn deeply from the bottom of your stomach and great big tears come into your eyes. This is the shift that signifies that your body's involuntary muscles are being mobilized. Your involuntary nervous system is coming into play. Yawning or tearing is most often accompanied by a complete letting go. It is a total releasing of all burdens such as caused by physical stress, mental rigidity, and spiritual limitations.

Now you are free from the all-encompassing prison of the mind cocoon. You are like a butterfly that has finally achieved the freedom of the sky. Your bodily movements are unhindered. So go on and let your body enjoy the unrestricted ease and mobility to which it has a right. Spend as much time as you want allowing your body to flow with katsugen.

Do not be dismayed at what your body will do, the movements that it will flow into. The body is capable of many movements that you have not allowed it to do until now. Let it make those movements. Sometimes your body will move gracefully, sometimes it will be jerky. Sometimes it will match the beat of the music, sometimes it will be disjointed and not fit the beat of the music at all. Whatever. It is okay. Your body will not harm itself as long as you are practicing katsugen correctly. It is when you are dancing or doing athletics that injuries happen. That is because your mind forces your body to comply with its directions. When doing katsugen, there is no forcing. The movements have nothing to do with any mind-made rules. The only rules it will follow are the rules of the Innate Bodily Intelligence.

Remember when you were a child? Or, if not, go to a playground and look at young children playing. They skip, hop, jump and allow their body to move as it wants without self-consciousness or inhibitions. It is only when they grow up that they lose this freedom. As they age, adults tell them what actions are proper and what actions aren't. That is how people imprison their body with their minds. Once into katsugen, you can act as a child again, but since you are not a child, your movements will be less active. But don't prematurely decide how to move, your body will know.

Let your body move itself.

Expressing the joy of breathing, of motion, of being, of life itself is usually the first step. These expressions are graceful and are aesthetically pleasing. Many people have entered this level completely on their own.

The next level of releasing debilitating emotional toxins come when you are able to express anger, sadness, frustration, jealousy, irritation, hatred, stress, pain, etc., in other words, the negative energies. This is a more difficult state to achieve, because it means that you have to tap into the aspects of yourself that you have been trying to suppress. This level of katsugen can induce movements that make you belch, yawn, your eyes tear, and your nose run. This is an important level to achieve because it is a sign that your involuntary nervous system is being exercised.

Think of the movement of the body we call the "shudder". We shudder at things with which we are disgusted, irritated, fearful of, and sad about. The shudder is the body's way of releasing the emotional toxins that is related to the thoughts of those things that affected us negatively. In a way, think of katsugen as one big, extended shudder. A shudder that is done by all parts of the body, in various ways, using different movements and vibrations; fast, slow, graceful, jerky, etc.

Basically, you allow all the emotions that you have within you to flow through and out of you by manifesting it in motion.

Just keep your mind away from it. This is not to say that the mind becomes unconscious. The mind should be there, relaxed but consciously watching, not hindering the body's movements whatsoever, ready to step in if the body wanders off into doing dangerous things.

Sort of like an adult watching children at play. Relaxed and detached but still keeping an eye on them. Have fun. Enjoy the exuberance of letting your body move in total freedom.

SPONTANEITY OF MOVEMENTS

> *"Your heart beats without thinking,*
> *you breathe with no thought.*
> *Your body knows the truth,*
> *'though your mind is stuck on meanings."*

There are no set movements in katsugen as there are in Tai Chi, yoga and aerobics. There are movements, though, that some people repeat on a regular basis. This is probably because that person's body uses that particular movement to relieve a certain stress. Wringing of the hands is common, as is the rolling of the neck and swaying of the body.

When katsugen has been properly induced, the autonomic nervous system of the body will begin to show itself. The yawn is the primary involuntary action that will occur, along with tearing of the eyes and the running of the nose, although I have also experienced belching and breaking wind as part of the body's natural response to katsugen. If one is ill or has an unbalanced condition, it is not uncommon for that person to want to throw up or use the bathroom. These involuntary responses are important. They signify that katsugen is allowing the body freedom to move as it sees fit. When practicing katsugen with other people, it is practically a knee-jerk reaction to stifle these bodily functions. Suppress them if you have to, but always remember to let it go when practicing katsugen in private.

Allow katsugen to affect the whole body, even your vocal chords. Sometimes there will be a desire to yell, holler or sing. Do it. Again, throw self-consciousness out the door and let fly with nonsense syllables, growls, screams, laughs, etc. Get it all out of your system.

It is like primal scream therapy except that verbal expression, hollering and screaming can only go so far in relieving the deep traumas and stress that we have collected in our body. Katsugen exercise releases stress built up in our muscle memory over many years.

The whole point is to gain control by letting go of control. It sounds easy, but many find it hard to do. They have been taught and conditioned since childhood that unusual movements and uncontrolled bodily motions are inappropriate, indecorous and definitely not for those who are civilized and respected. Their minds are completely dominating their bodies. This means that whatever creativity there is that springs from the body spontaneously is stifled and repressed and the total self is unbalanced.

Is it really that difficult to go against our conditioning? Here's a story that may illustrate the resistance that people have against what they have been taught as proper. I once took an American friend to a Japanese noodle restaurant. The Japanese love their noodles and like to eat it by slurping noisily. They say that it tastes better that way because the flavor of the soup is more exposed to the taste buds by the action of the slurping. So, I encouraged my friend to slurp. He listened to my explanation with interest but didn't venture forth immediately into a frenzy of slurping. It was evident to me that he had been taught that slurping is bad manners and that he couldn't go against the conditioning just like that. It was only after I asked him if he just wasn't capable of slurping that he showed me that he could by giving the noodles one token slurp. But that was it. Just one slurp. How deep and ingrained our childhood conditioning is!

The conditioning against the movements that will arise from katsugen is the same. But unlike slurping, the katsugen movements are more basic to us. They are part of our body and usually only lightly covered up by conditioning and learned behavior. All that is required to unleash this potential is to practice letting go the dominance of the dictatorial mind through regular katsugen.

There are different levels of letting go. Going from the normal mode of everyday activities such as working, reading, watching TV, etc., to dancing is one level. Going from dancing to the initial stage of katsugen is the next level. From there to the vibratory state of katsugen is another level. And from the vibratory state to the yawning state another level. It is difficult to precisely delineate these levels because they will often overlap.

Level One – the normal state of activity

Level Two – dancing, aerobics, free-form exercise

Level Three – initial katsugen state: freely swaying and moving with the purpose of getting autonomic nervous system response

Level Four – vibratory state, highly vigorous state

Level Five – yawning, belching, shuddering, vigorous movement etc.: the autonomic nervous system fully responding

In a period of practicing katsugen for fifteen to thirty minutes, all of these levels may be manifested progressively but sometimes the movement will regress from the Five and Four levels to Three and Two. Although levels Four and Five are where we want to get to, it is okay to shift into all of the levels. Allow the body to decide how long it wants to stay at a certain level.

Katsugen often results in many original and creative moves that can be used in dancing. It is an excellent way to explore all the diversity of movements that our body will come up with. Such as it is, it is tempting for a dancer to use katsugen to come up with new moves. The problem with this is that once we begin to become self-conscious of our katsugen moves, the mind starts to take over again, and it no longer is completely katsugen; it becomes a mix of katsugen and dancing. At this point, please be careful, the body and the mind will become confused as to what is what with the result that injury may occur. If you want to explore dance using katsugen, I suggest that you become aware of the difference between the two. Be able to shift from one to the other, being aware that that is what you are doing. In this way, there is no confusion between mind and body. But I suggest strongly that it is preferable and safer to just do katsugen by itself, letting the body move in a myriad of ways, and remembering the moves so that you can reference it later when you want to dance.

I have found in teaching katsugen that many people think they have already reached that state when they have not. Ladies, in particular, often get into Level Three and think that that is all there is. They make graceful, gentle and easy motions with their bodies, swaying to and fro. This level of movement is good, but one must always remember that this is but the initial stage of katsugen. One of the goals of katsugen is to release pent up stress, frustrations, anger, discontent, spite, fury, hatred, etc. These are very volatile and excitable energies. To think that one can release these energies through gentle, graceful motions is being naive. What comes in must go out. The more volatile the energy that is disturbing you, the more energetic the release of that energy will be. That is why the vibratory stage is achieved. This is akin to a great big, prolonged shudder, except that it may happen to your whole body as well as to individual parts of it, such as the hand, arm, leg, etc. During this vibratory stage, the body's movement can vary from gentle swaying and rocking to hand or leg wringing, jumping up and down, thrusting out of arms and legs, rolling around on the floor, rapid shaking of the head and various other movements, most of them completely spontaneous and original.

This is why I recommend that katsugen be initially practiced privately. No matter how uninhibited and without self-conscious thinking you think you are, you will, in the beginning, be hesitant about doing in public those things which you might feel free to do in private.

There is another important thing to remember. Although the mind ceases domination of the body, the mind is still conscious and in potential control. The body is "on a leash and taken out for a walk," so to speak, and the mind is always ready and able to step in and take over if it is necessary.

Katsugen is NOT doing "everything and anything you want to do." Katsugen is allowing just the body to move as it wants to. First of all, the body only wants to do certain bodily things. Katsugen is allowing the body to do those things. The mind, if it is allowed to do "anything and everything", can be dangerous because it has an ego with its potential for destructive behavior and misplaced energy. The body can only do those things which nature has built within it, and without an ego, it is but a docile pet, which must be kept on the leash of the mind when "taken out for a walk."

CLOSING THE MOVEMENT

Eventually, your body will cease its movements. Or sometimes you will have to halt the movement because of your schedule.

To close katsugen, get back into your original posture, the position you were in when you were inducting katsugen.

With spine straight and hands on your lap, breathe out and relax, keeping your mind on your tanden. Give a great big sigh, say or think, "aaaahhh", as you relax.

Repeat three times.

Relax. Katsugen is closed.

After katsugen, your body is in a delicate state. If possible, do not do anything strenuous or active for a few minutes. Just stay still and meditate.

Think of all the millions of cells in your body and how happy they are that they had time to play and be free. At the end of your meditation, resume your normal activity. If your mind is still foggy, you may require additional time to relax and come back into a normal state.

NOTE: Katsugen releases toxins out of your body. These toxins may not only be physical but also mental and emotional. In some people the surfacing of these toxins may create nausea or emotional distress. If this happens to you, do not worry. Rather, feel relieved that those poisons are being ejected. Repeated practice should eradicate all toxins in a few days after which you will feel light, unburdened and healthier than you've ever been!

TEN POINTS TO REMEMBER DURING KATSUGEN

1. To learn katsugen exercise, you can practice it with those who know the induction movements, but because the practice induces bodily functions that may be embarrassing, practicing in private often may be necessary to actualize full potential. Once you have become comfortable with the flow, practicing katsugen with others may result in additional benefits, such as the augmentation of each other's ki (qi/chi).

2. Relax your mind and body. Abandon all thoughts of embarrassment and self-consciousness.

3. Just move your body any way you feel.

4. Keep your mind away from your body. Free your body from the dictations of your mind.

5. Your mind should be conscious, and in potential control, yet distant and not controlling, ready to step in anytime if it is needed.

6. Try to stay away from "dance moves" if it is not natural.

7. Tearing and running of the nose is an important signal that you are inducing katsugen. Allow it to happen.

8. Flow into and enjoy those bodily actions and movements. Relinquish control of it.

9. When you feel all the nervous energy you've pent up wanting to get out, let it. Move, shake, stretch, whatever.

10. Let it go. Enjoy katsugen as it flows. Renew yourself.

As you identify with your body,
you hone your skills and strengthen your health.

As you identify with your mind,
you further your knowledge and intelligence.

As you identify with your spirit,
you grow in love and wisdom.

As you identify with all three,
your soul becomes a fine instrument of God.

THE LIFESTYLE AND PHILOSOPHY OF KATSUGEN

It is simple. Health, wisdom and happiness are essential parts of each and every one of us that have been covered up by our own fears, doubts and negativity. To achieve optimum health, wisdom and happiness, one has merely to release this wellspring of divinity within us. It is a relaxing. A re-opening up of the dynamic self given to us by the Source. We were all created through the love of this universe itelligence and so we all have a part of this essence within us. It is only through acceptance of the spirituality within us that we can become whole, an intrinsic oneness of universal wisdom, beauty and love.

Why do people become unhealthy, foolish and unhappy when we all have this universal essence within us?

We have free will so that we can love without being forced to; love of family, of friends, mates, siblings, etc. After all, what is love if it is not given freely? How meaningless love would be if we could not do so under our own free will?

Unfortunately, this free will can also create problems. Free will means freedom to make our own choices and decisions, and many people choose to be led by negative thoughts. Fear and doubt are the number one nemesis to love and acceptance.

So many people are immobile in their lives. They are paralyzed by fear. Fear of rejection, fear of failure, fear of having done wrong (shame and guilt), fear of success, fear of criticism, fear of being different, fear of the past, fear of the unknown and much, much more. This fear is supported by doubts: doubt of their own self-worth, doubt of their divine nature, doubt of the friendliness of the universe, doubt that they are being loved.

Where do these fears and doubts come from?

They come from the external, material world and into our minds. Negative events that happen to a person imprint that person's worldview and shape his/her image of the world and of the self. The world teaches fear and doubt, and all too often, we are avid learners.

One of the tools used to counter the world's negative messages is affirmation. There have been many books on this subject. Affirmations are positive messages that we read or say to ourselves that reinforce our own assertions of confidence, self-worth, and validity. I will elaborate more about affirmations in a later chapter. Affirmations are great and they have certainly been efficacious in keeping my mind on the positive, but they are only partially effective if they are limited to just the mind.

For instance, no matter how often we tell ourselves that the universe is friendly, if the physical world keeps beating us up, our physical body will never believe that it is so. Affirmations, in order to be effective to our entire self, must go beyond the mental, to encompass the physical and spiritual aspects of our being.

In order for our total being to acknowledge that the universe is a friendly, loving place to be, we have to be able to experience the universe's friendliness and love with all aspects of self; physical, mental and spiritual.

Many people find this hard to do. Why? Because, to fully experience love, friendship, truth, and all the transcendental attributes of higher reality, we must first remove out of the way such debilitating attributes as fear, distrust, guilt, closed mindedness, envy, hate, shame, cynicism, insecurity and other manifestations of negative experiences that originated in the past. In order to accept and appreciate the positive universal values that are being constantly bestowed upon us, we have to be open and free and unified as a being. We have to be in a state of acceptance, one and whole. As the masters of Zen say, "one cannot receive with a clenched fist."

It comes down to achieving a mindset based on the freedom of the self, in a sense, spiritual liberty. A state where one can be totally accepting, totally flexible, totally free. Once we can match the freedom of our body and mind to the freedom of our spirit, we can be free in totality. Within that completeness of freedom lies the natural beauty, love and well-being that is inherently ours. Going home to this freedom is the purpose of katsugen.

For optimum well-being, I recommend the three-fold path of service (to oneself and others), prayer (including affirmations), and worshipful meditation (connecting to the Source). This will ensure the balance of body, mind and soul for creating a healthy, fulfilled and happy life.

In a nutshell, the philosophy of katsugen is to be secure in faith that the universe is friendly, and that you are blessed with all that is needed to be happy and be productive. From that faith comes the vital energy to focus on the goodness in our lives rather than to be bogged down by seeing only the negative. This philosophy of well-being can be used in all aspects of life: from physical activities such as athletics to intellectual pursuits such as education, writing and science; to the arts such as music and painting to spiritual ventures of worship and meditation.

All that is needed to put this philosophy into action is to maintain a balance of motion; to achieve a dynamic circulation of the energies inherent in that field of endeavor.

The practice of katsugen is but one way of balancing and maintaining the energies that act on our bodies. There are many out there such as Tai Chi, yoga, Feldenkrais, aerobics, the martial arts, athletics, etc. It is up to each one of us to find one or several that are best suited for our individual needs.

The rest of this book deals with the katsugen lifestyle and how it relates to the various aspects of our lives. The ideas and opinions expressed are by no means conclusive; rather, they are observations on my part that are constantly evolving into newer and broader insights. My suggestion is that you use this information as you see fit, to evolve personal insights that further your own total health and well-being.

Self-discipline
is self-administered pain.

If you discipline yourself,
the universe won't have to do it for you.

ஐ

In a universe of contrasts such as we live in,
pain and suffering is a vivid and horrifying
experience.
But it is only because
we live in such a world of contrasts
that beauty and ecstasy
are also sharply and gloriously defined.

五

THE PURPOSE OF PAIN

Pain is a survival mechanism. Pain tells us not to do those things that are causing the pain. As an infant, we might unwisely put our hand in a fire. The resulting pain tells us *not* to do that again. It is experiential wisdom. We learn that fire equals heat, equals pain, equals "don't put hand in the fire"; a very simple equation. Pain is a signpost telling us which paths to avoid. Pain doesn't tell us what is right, it tells us what is wrong.

To use an analogy, think of skiing. To learn how to ski we often fall, which is painful. Falling makes us learn how to ski better, but wanting to fall does not make for a better skier. The purpose is to learn how to ski masterfully *without* falling. When we're not falling anymore, it means we have learned. When we can lead our life so that we do not make ourselves suffer, we have mastered the art of living.

That does not mean that there will no longer be mistakes and errors that might cause some pain. When we become expert at skiing, we may start challenging more difficult slopes, maybe even to the extreme. Then, pain and suffering may again be experienced in trying to achieve a more demanding goal that we have set for ourselves.

To live a life where we experience pain and suffering daily may mean that we are making regular errors in judgment. Whereas to live so that we do not suffer at all may mean that we are not challenging ourselves to the utmost. It is a fine line. A matter of balance.

Balance your life. After you sit in front of a computer and work your brain for a few hours, go outside and work your body for a few hours. It doesn't have to be strenuous, just get out there and let your body move.

After you use your eyes to read, balance it by listening to some music. When you run, balance that with swimming. When you work your finger to the bone, take time off to have some fun. Balance is absolutely necessary for well-being. Balance is a universal constant. If you don't balance your life, the universe will do it for you, except that when the universal forces take over, you will suffer from the abrupt shift as you are mercilessly thrown about at its whim.

For instance, when one is overworked, the equilibrium swiftly asserts itself. The physical system that enables you to work shuts down and you will get a cold or some other illness. Conversely, when one overindulges in pleasures, the system that enables you to have pleasure shuts down, and pleasures become meaningless. The key is to have the mindfulness to balance your life before the universe does it for you.

That doesn't mean that you should use a clock to time everything you do and make sure you give every activity equal time. Not at all. By practicing katsugen, or even just by simply listening to your body, you will intuitively know what to do to balance your life. Pain is a sure indicator that your activity should be shifted to something other than what is causing the pain.

Self-improvement can also cause pain. "No Pain, No Gain" is a masochistic way of achieving goals, but it's easy to see how this kind of thinking came about.

Exercising can be painful, especially when we are pushing ourselves beyond our comfort zone. To acquire knowledge is often painful; studying and researching long hours is a pain. So is finding out a well-kept secret about yourself or someone you love. Pain can be involved when trying to improve in any endeavor, physical, intellectual or emotional. But there is also pain in not improving or staying ignorant. How painful it is to be at a standstill when everyone else is progressing!

Therefore, pain can happen when there is resistance between where you are and to where you're going. From ignorance to knowledge, illness to health, from discomfort to comfort, from stasis to movement, all involves some pain.

So, can one improve without pain? I say, yes. Gradual improvement over time is painless and often pleasurable. I would go so far as to say that gradual improvement is more beneficial in that it is long lasting and is more quality oriented. It is trying to improve too quickly, or gaining too much knowledge too rapidly that produces pain. For those who are competitive athletes, or those who wish to "get there quickly", the way of pain may be a valid path, but I do not believe it is necessarily a desirable course for all who wish to improve.

Noguchi-san used to say that health is not a state of feeling no pain, but rather, the fact that you can feel pain means you are, in a sense, healthy. When you get hit, you bruise so that more blood rushes to the point of injury and nurses the damaged cells. When you catch an infection, you get a fever because the theory is that the increase in temperature makes it more difficult for the germs to survive. These symptoms are natural functions of your body's defense and warning system, just like pain.

So it would be a mistake to think that any health practice is going to enable you to maintain a state where there is no instability of your health. Rather, having your ups and downs is the healthy thing.

In *The Wisdom of the Body*, Dr. Sherwin B. Nuland writes:

"A stable system is not a system that never changes. It is a system that constantly and instantly adjusts and readjusts in order to maintain such a state of being that all necessary functions are permitted to operate at maximum efficiency. Stability demands change to compensate for changing circumstances. Ultimately, then, stability depends on instability."

The key is not necessarily to totally avoid disease or injury, because those things are often unavoidable, but being able to constantly and instantly adjust to them and recover from them. If one were to not be exposed to germs over an extended period, one would not get sick, but then, since the body cannot strengthen its immune system through exposure with those germs, it would get deathly ill if it got exposed after that time.

A body that is ideally in tune would, upon exposure to a germ, develop immunity to it before the symptoms show up. I've had experiences when I felt a cold coming on and a tickle in my throat, but ejected whatever was causing it with one tremendous sneeze, and never came down with any symptoms. The germs were not all gone from me, I am sure, but my immune system had thrown out a great deal of them and kept the rest to be used to make antibodies against.

Is this possible? It has worked for me and many others. Will it work for you? It is certainly an ideal worth striving through katsugen.

Physical.
Mental.
Spiritual.
Three aspects of my total.

When all three
become one.
I have truly begun.

If you've see one
you've seen them all.
For they are inseparable.

PHYSICAL EXERCISE

Katsugen is a physical exercise, but it's intent is neither aerobic nor anaerobic. In this chapter I would like to discuss the activities that people often think of as being physical exercise: athletics.

There are those who take to athletics readily and there are those who hardly exercise at all. Katsugen can help both types of individuals. Those who have a problem with exercising will discover a new perspective in its approach, while those who are athletes will find that practicing katsugen will result in better coordination and a way to prevent injuries.

Sports and athletics began as exercises to prepare for the hardships of war. We hardened ourselves for living in a hell-like environment (war) by pushing our bodies to the breaking point and by creating conditions of mental competition and strife in a game. This tradition still continues. Football is like a small-scale war. Even tennis is similar to a duel. All competition is an effort to defeat another human being or our self.

War is becoming less and less acceptable. People are discovering that cooperation is more productive than competition. Which means that there are many who do not want to train for war, but still desire to remain fit. So is it possible to train for cooperation rather than competition? To exercise in preparation for a peaceful life rather than for a warlike life? Definitely, yes!

To exercise in preparation for competition means we have to push our body to its limits. The purpose of that is to try to become stronger than one's competitor. To exercise for cooperation means we exercise our body for the joy of living in a friendly world. An added benefit is that we stay healthy and we are more able to contribute to the welfare of the whole, rather than the part. For instance, running every day in order to be faster than others, or faster than your previous time is competitive. Competition is fine. When one is in good shape and skilled at a sport, there is nothing like competition. Competition is exhilarating and to triumph is a joy. However, there is a difference between the cooperative mindset and the competitive mindset. To exercise regularly so that one can feel good, be healthy and an asset to ones' family and associates is cooperative. It is a great difference, not only mentally, but also emotionally, spiritually and in the sense of well-being that it can give us.

I used to hate to run when I was in grade school. It wasn't exercising that I disliked, because I loved to swim, but I was a slow runner and the last one around the track, and that was what I detested. Then, when I was in my early adulthood, I found a book called "The Zen of Running" by Fred Rohe. In it, he said, "There are no standards and no possible victories except the joy you are living while dancing your run.... you are not running for some future reward-the real reward is now!" The book described the joy of running just for the sake of it. Not for competition, not to lose weight, not for any particular reason except for sheer joy.

I realized that the reason I hated to run was because I had it in my mind that I had to keep on running even when I wanted to stop. Somehow and somewhere, I was conditioned to think that I had to set as a goal to run, a certain distance or a span of time, like, for instance, I had to run two miles or for 20 minutes, three times a week or something similar. I was competing with myself. Fred Rohe presented me with another perspective. Run for joy and pleasure. I just ran, and as soon as it became a chore, I stopped, and resumed only when I wanted to start running again. Run only when it causes pleasure and I will want to run again, and again, until my running ability increases to the point where I can run for many minutes without pain.

The reason why so many people cannot continue their regimen of exercise is because they set a certain goal that becomes too painful to attain; they compete with themselves. They are able to bear the pain for a week, maybe two, a couple of months even, but eventually the pain becomes too much and they quit, because to them, running has been associated with pain. Running becomes pain.

Of course, there are those who are blessed with a certain athleticism so that their experience with running is not painful and they can continue over the years with little trouble. But even they may have problems in another field of exercise, such as swimming, or skiing, climbing, lifting weights, or whatever. There are only a few people who are so athletically endowed that they are good at every sport in which they engage.

For those of you who rarely exercise, katsugen will rejuvenate the desire to move your body. Once you have that desire, go out there and just have fun. Go for a walk, a leisurely swim, jog a little. But always come back from it with memories of pleasure. As soon as you overdo it, and it becomes a painful or uncomfortable experience, the desire to go back out there will be erased by the association of that activity to pain. Keep it an enjoyable experience and you will continue to want to do it over and over again. Exercise to enjoy life, not as a competitive endeavor.

Let me tell you, though, that it's not necessarily that easy. After reading that book by Fred Rohe, I started to run, going about it with only joy in mind. But as soon as I began to get a little better at running, I started to push myself, running longer and faster, until it became a chore. It wasn't soon after that I stopped altogether.

There is something about us, humans, that are competitive. If we aren't trying to beat someone else, we are trying to beat ourselves. We are always setting goals with our minds and coercing our bodies to reach it. This is fine. That innate quality within us is what makes us different from animals. It has given us science, technology and all the wonders of civilization. But it has also given us war and crime as well as environmental degradation and social strife.

The purpose of katsugen is to keep the competitiveness but at the same time to control it and to even turn it off once in a while for balance, so that we can enjoy life for the sake of living. As Fred Rohe said, "...you are not running for some future reward-the real reward is now!" The bottom line is to exercise to feel good. As soon as it becomes painful, too fatiguing, or results in constant discomfort, stop and re-evaluate your regimen. Consult a professional if necessary.

There is another problem here, though, that I found myself faced with. Which is that in listening to my body, when do I know if it's being lazy or not? Will my body become slothful if I let it do what it wants?

I believe that for the most part, the body is not innately lazy or slothful. Those feelings of laziness come from not enough sleep, being overworked, taking poisons into our body such as alcohol and nicotine, insufficient proper nutrition, lack of exercise, injuries and other external factors. But our lives being what it is, we still need to deal with these conditions of dissipated energy, which is what laziness is. The best thing to do is to get enough sleep and rest, quit ingesting the poisons, eat the proper foods, exercise and/or heal the injury. When that is not easily done, we resort to mental discipline or drugs to force our bodies into doing what we want it to do, and the cycle continues.

Using katsugen, the cycle can be broken, but this is where we must depart from the arena of the physical to the other aspects of our total self.

When we speak of physical exercise, we often leave out the other components that make up the totality of who we are; the mind and spirit. We are not just a mechanical body with a bio-computer. The computer that is our brain has an intangible mind and the mind itself is indwelt by a spirit. This ties in directly with techniques that deal with the mindal and spiritual aspects of our selves and is covered in chapters further on.

Glimpses of a world that I want you to see;
beautiful facets refracting light.

Life is a diamond, a jewel in the dark.
Emitting the colors of divine inspiration.

Sparkling brilliantly aglow.

七

CREATIVITY

What does it mean to create? To produce something totally original? Solomon said, *"Nihil novi sub sola"* (*"There is nothing new under the sun."*) Our scientists confirm this with the Law of Conservation of Matter and Energy which states that matter and energy cannot be created or destroyed, but can only change form, meaning that the total quantity of matter and energy available in the universe is a fixed amount and never any more or less. As far as we know, nothing truly new can be created by the hand of man.

When we talk of creativity, we are actually speaking of converting one form to another, with a result that seems entirely new to the perception of the viewer. An unprecedented piece of visual art, an invention, a revolutionary idea, a novel literary work, innovative music, all may appear original but are not. They are but forms that have been drastically changed from the previous patterns that have come before. They only *appear* new and original to those who are unaware of the source of the idea that gave rise to that result.

God can be truly creative; to create something from nothing, but to us humans, to be creative means to be able to arrange something into a form which is far distant from the original; to be able to take a quantum leap into forms previously unimagined by other mortals. What makes this so difficult for many is that most people are stuck in existing forms. They have been conditioned by society into accepting currents forms of thinking and behavior as the norm and are afraid to venture out into new forms that may be unacceptable. After all, new forms of thinking and behavior are often thought of as being "bizarre" and "strange" before being accepted in a positive light and then labeled "revolutionary" or "innovative".

When we are children we are often more creative because we are not limited by previous concepts. As we grow older, we become more conditioned into accepting what is right and proper and as we age we become more concerned about protecting what we already have rather than trying to form something new. As a result, creativity wanes and sometimes often disappears in adults. Stagnation steps in and we are dead.

Katsugen can revive the creativity. Society conditions the mind, and the mind conditions the body into actions that it considers proper. Katsugen allows the body to once again move and act in the ways nature meant it to act. This freedom that the body regains translates into the mind questioning its self-restraint. With suitable encouragement in the form of positive affirmations, the mind will again become creative.

To learn, to study, and to memorize takes focus and effort. It is a striving. To be creative, to bring forth new thoughts, new ideas, and new ways of doing things requires a relaxation, an opening up. This is what katsugen does.

Transmuting Negative Energy Into Positive Energy

When we have strong emotional feelings attached to a past experience, especially in regards to adverse circumstances in life that were particularly stressful, horrifying or extremely uncomfortable, those emotions can affect our life in undesirable ways. Those past experiences may have happened in times of war, illness and other personal crises.

It has been advised by many that the best way to deal with these negative emotions is to channel them into something constructive. Emotions stemming from, say, a wartime experience may be channeled into a book recounting that experience; or into a song, a play or maybe just into leading a better life. Negative emotions can be channeled into something positive. This is good advice.

However, what may be difficult is to tame those wild emotions so that it can be handled and structured into a positive endeavor. When the emotions are extremely strong, the mind often rebels at looking at the very root of those emotions as it may cause dismay and discomfort. Since those emotions are like a dormant volcano, with powerful energies waiting to be activated, one must be very careful in releasing that energy so that it does not become destructive or haphazard.

Katsugen tames this energy so that it can be channeled safely and utilized in beneficial ways. In physical practice and philosophy, katsugen can transmute negative energy into positive, turning evil into good.

By changing the negative emotions that we may have into movement, we slowly bleed away the excess energy, the potentially destructive force that may be churning inside, making us seethe with uncontrollable emotions and feelings. The physical movements of katsugen turn the raw negative energies into a positive activity. After much of the excess energies have been released, the remaining emotions are easier to deal with, as the edgy fierceness has been trimmed. Then, one can, more comfortably, begin to channel what is left into something creative.

Spiritually, we can use the same principle to transmute evil energy into good energy, to return good for evil, to "turn the other cheek." By releasing the emotional blockage of our evil feelings by expressing and letting go of them through harmless physical movement, we can uncover the inner divinity within us so that it can shine out, being no longer impeded by negative emotions.

Who am I?
What will I be?
These questions keep bugging me.

八

WORK, STRESS AND RELAXATION

Some people love their work while others hate it. Most of us are somewhere in the middle. We put up with it but wish we could win the lottery so we could retire.

A question that I ask those who express such a desire is, "What would you do right now, if you were filthy rich and could do anything you want?"

The answer I've gotten were typically something like, "Go party!" Then I would say, "Well, you could do that right now without being rich."

Then they would think a bit and come up with buying a new car, house, a boat, private plane, going on a world cruise, etc. Then I would ask, "After you've finished buying everything you want and been around the world a couple of times, then what?"

This usually leaves them shrugging and hemming and hawing after which they say, "Well, I'll think of something. Figuring that out is a problem I'd love to have."

What does this have to do with katsugen? Well, after practicing the body, mind and soul art of katsugen for a while, it's like being a billionaire. You are free to do anything you want. Of course, the money may not be there, but having money is not liberating unless you know how to spend your time in a worthwhile manner.

By opening up to the creative and divine potential within, one can tailor one's life so that it is meaningful, interesting, challenging, vital, and fun without having a lot of wealth.

It's funny how we often think of work as doing something unpleasant, while doing something we enjoy is not really considered work. When someone we know has a job that seems pleasurable, people will often comment and ask, "When is he going to get a *real* job?" The truth is, work does not have to be an unwelcome chore. In fact, real work, work that is done with the full focus of heart and soul is extremely enjoyable.

I heard a story once that a survey was taken of one hundred students in college. They were asked if they were going to shape their career around doing something they enjoyed doing, or something that would make them money regardless of their particular liking for that occupation. About ten percent said they would do what pleased them, while 90 percent went the other route. Well, thirty years later, a follow-up survey found out that most of the ten percent that worked on what they enjoyed were very successful, while the others were dissatisfied with their life.

People who truly enjoy their work are out there. I know many who do and they are not just artists, musicians, actors and sports personalities who have jobs that appear to be fun.

So how does one use katsugen to get joy out of work?

Most of us, at one time or another, must work at something we do not enjoy. This is one of those immutable facts of life. Jobs like that are usually stepping-stones to better work. Katsugen can relieve the stress so that you can stay working at an unpleasant job until it's time to move on to your heart's desire. Or better still, move on to that better job now.

Some people are stuck in jobs that they detest and don't know how to get out of it. They think that if they quit they will be out on the street. That there family will disown them. That they will never work again. Such anxiety! Katsugen frees you to go where you want to go, to do what you want to do, by vanquishing the fear that has settled into your body; the fear that has manifested as society's commands to conform to an illusory standard.

Once the body has been freed, the mind becomes more creative, and work becomes a project that you want to pursue, rather than a job you must do in order to survive.

Some people are lucky. They were never conditioned to have to walk lockstep in tune to an imaginary society's rules, but they are the few. Many are conditioned by the past history of the human race. How many millennia have our ancestors lived as chattel, serfs, servants, peons, and slaves? I would say that the majority of people in all of history had to live at the beck and call of those in higher authority. Work for those being ground under by the oppressor's heel was rarely pleasant. It has only been recently that a larger percentage of the world's population has had the luxury of choosing which work to engage in. No wonder that many still think of work as a chore and a burden: harsh, unpleasant, and unnecessarily tiring.

Well, free yourself from that concept. You don't have to work at something you hate, dislike or want to put in the past anymore. The philosophy of katsugen is that you have within yourself something of innate value that you can manifest in your life. Go with freedom in the direction your heart leads you. Release yourself from enslavement by the hooks of anxiety and seeming limitations.

Freedom is within you. Allow it to manifest itself.

Even if you consider yourself free and are working at something you love, stress may still be inevitable. A sure sign that you are overstressed is when your heart is no longer in your work. Whatever effort you put out seems to have no meaning. Your interest is flagging and you can't seem to concentrate on those things that you found so fascinating before.

Remember that freedom means you can choose to cease your work. However, too much stress from being engrossed in work can confuse our ego/mind. We can mistakenly be caught up in the concept that our value and worth is directly a result of the work we do, so that we tie in our insecurities to our work, saying to ourselves (often sub-consciously) *if I don't finish this I will never achieve my goals, my boss, my fellow workers and my family will not respect me,* etc. It is a mistake for work to become the criteria for self-worth and self-respect. Work is important, and we should do it well, but our value and worth should go beyond work. We are valuable as friends, as parents, as siblings, as a *person,* regardless of the periodic success, or its lack, at work. Sometimes we are successful, sometimes we are not. Stress comes from relating our successes or our failures with self-importance. Keep our egos out of it and we can work stress free. And by becoming stress free the less vulnerable our egos become.

When one is stressed, freedom is bound up by knots of goal achievement dictated by the ego/mind. When caught up in work, how difficult it is to even sit for a moment without thinking: *I have to get this done, I have to get that done, the deadline is tomorrow, so and so will be upset if this isn't finished, etc.* Our minds are constantly prodding us into action. Stress is a result of this mental pressure in conflict with what our soul really wants to do.

Obviously, the key to relieving stress is relaxation. There are many ways to relax. Sleeping is important but one can sleep and not feel rested if the mind is still active during sleep. I believe that allowing the soul to make decisions is the best way to deal with work and stress. In using the word *soul*, I am referring to the essence of your humanity, incorporating the body, mind and spirit. It is the purest and best part of you, the distillation of all that you have learned in your life.

See if you can differentiate between what your mind wants to do and what your soul wants to do. The mind is caught up with deadlines, accomplishments and material gain. The soul is interested in spiritual benefits, personal relationships, health and oneness with the universe. The mind (with ego) gets involved in competition, the soul engenders cooperation. The mind strives to grasp, the soul relaxes in order to give and receive.

Make it a practice to allowing your soul to decide your actions. Ignore the ego/mind's incessant clamoring for getting things done. This will be difficult for many. There are things your mind tells you to do that simply must be done, you say. You have to get up to go to work, you must work according to your job's requirements, you have to do this, and you have to do that. Sure, you must do those things to keep your paycheck coming and your life in order, but once in a while, whether it's once a day, once a week or once a month, practice doing what your soul *really* wants to do.

Actually, many people do this naturally. They may call it veggieing out or just simply loafing around doing nothing. These times of doing "nothing" are actually very valuable. They are a direct reaction to overwork and stress. The problem is, people think it's a bad thing and don't do it often enough or long enough.

It's a well-known fact that many people do not get enough sleep. Not only do they not get enough sleep, most people do not get enough rest. By this, I mean the time you spend awake just reflecting on the past, feeling relaxed and unhurried, enjoying the present, listening to the birds sing and smelling the flowers.

These moments are truly vital to one's well-being. These occasions are when we take stock of our lives, replenish our desire for living, breathe in the sweet air of just living and realize the value of our lives. They give meaning and value to the work we have accomplished in the past, and give us a sense of where we want to go in the future.

It is not necessarily easy to get into this state and stay there as long as needed. In fact, when we go through an extended time of working very hard, it can be difficult to make the transition into being fully relaxed. And often, once we get there, we don't stay there long enough. We feel as if we are wasting our time, when actually, we are, in effect, stopping time so that we have a chance to breathe in and appreciate the life that we worked so hard to achieve.

So how do we know if we are truly in this state and how long we should stay there? First of all, you are in this state when you realize that you are totally free to do whatever you want. You are free from doing all those things that are a part of your regular schedule, whether it's work, exercise, luncheons, social service, even regimented play. When you can sit down and know that you don't have to do anything you don't really want to do that day, then you are completely free.

Stay in this level of relaxation long enough so that you begin to realize how stressed out you were before. It's so easy to fool yourself, once you've relaxed for a short time, into thinking that you are totally relaxed, but if you feel a bit of anxiety when thinking of work, you are not sufficiently relaxed.

Once you are totally relaxed, your creativity flourishes. Your activities spring from your soul. This will be work, but not work as you know it. In a sense, it will be play. It will be working at things you love to do.

Once this freedom becomes a part of one's life, engaging in activities that you love may become full time so that it replaces your previous work. Many people have done this, but the danger lies in that this playful work becomes too geared to making money and it becomes just like the work that you had gotten out of. The important thing to remember is to work with love and passion in mind, rather than money or profit.

Now is the time to remember,
now is the time to heed
the painstaking values created
with blood we had to bleed.

九

MEDICAL SCIENCE

The science of medicine has progressed in leaps and bounds in the last century. We live much longer and healthier now due to the benefits of medical science. But it is far from being infallible. As long as medical practitioners ignore or discount the presence of spirit and the effects of mind over the body, there will be a discrepancy between medical technique and the overcoming of disease.

Doctors and other medical persons are to be admired. They dedicate themselves to years and years of education and then go about fixing the ailments of the populace. Society is much indebted to their service and expertise.

Unfortunately, all is not well with the medical establishment. We read about malpractice suits, botched medical procedures, unscrupulous quacks and charlatans and other horrid medical stories all too often.

Maybe that is why many people resort to alternative health methods, of which katsugen is one. I think it is good that people are taking more responsibility for their own health. There are still many, though, that treat their body like their car. When it breaks down, they expect the doctor to fix it, just as they expect a mechanic to fix their car.

What's wrong with that?

First of all, a good mechanic knows all there is to know about a car, or if not, he can ask the manufacturer. No doctor, no matter how experienced, knows as much as he should know about the human body.

Secondly, each human body is different. Automobiles of each model type are basically all the same.

Thirdly, there is more to a human being than just the mechanical components; the whole must be treated rather than just the part. Holistic treatments have been around as alternative medicine for a long time but when will the medical establishment take a long, deep look at it and devote time and money into full-scale research and development? It's a shame that there is so little scientific knowledge regarding how the body, mind and spirit are interlinked. This paucity of information is why there are so few effective techniques to cure illnesses based on treating the person as one undivided whole.

Katsugen exercise is a preventative method and a way to use the natural power of self-healing within our bodily organism to regain health. It is holistic and very compatible with existing medical techniques. We can use katsugen to augment and assist the medical doctors that are caring for us. But there is one thing that is important to remember: the responsibility for our health lies upon each individual. Not the doctor. Not the alternative medical practitioner. Not our family. Each one us must take responsibility for his or her own health.

We must help our doctors. They are not supermen. They see many patients and they cannot devote as much time as they would like to each and every individual case. Each person and each medical condition is different. The most effective treatment would be custom tailored to each patient. If you are wealthy you can afford such personalized treatment. Most cannot. Since doctors will not have time to research each condition in detail, they resort to doing the best they can for the greatest number of people. They use drugs and treatment methods that are effective to the most amounts of people most of the time. If you happen to fit in to the class of people that respond well to the treatment, you are in luck. If not, well, the treatment doesn't work and you go looking elsewhere, possibly to another doctor or to a practitioner of alternative medicine.

It took me a long time to realize the above, but when I did, it seemed like an extremely haphazard way of maintaining health. I wanted expertise on my particular medical condition as it related to my mental and spiritual state and no one was providing me with it.

It became evident to me that my doctor did not have the time nor the desire to become an expert on my physical, mental, and spiritual health; that is, the total well-being of my entire self.

I discovered that there is only one person who can be that expert.

Me.

Katsugen exercise is the basic tool I use to stay in touch with my physical body. It keeps me aware and consciously linked to my autonomic nervous system through a series of feedback loops using bodily movements. This is extremely important because the autonomic nervous system is the oldest and most primitive part of our body's structure. It is the key to how the various parts of our body interact with each other. The cells, tissues, and organs signal each other through the autonomic nervous system in order to coordinate, stabilize, and balance their functions.

By using katsugen along with other techniques that enhance the well-being of the mind and soul (which I will mention in the chapter on mind and spirit), I can exist as a healthy, unified and integral whole. I become an expert on myself. So that when I do need to consult a doctor or health practitioner, I have the confidence to determine if their treatment for me is something that I think will be effective for me, not just physically, but in the totality of who I am.

Another tool that I found to be invaluable for maintaining health is the Internet. Researching the Internet can result in you becoming more knowledgeable about your condition than your doctor. After all, he has to research and study thousands of cases. You only have to study your own. Use this knowledge together with the knowledge you glean from living inside your body and your doctor's knowledge and have faith in yourself that you *can* manage and maintain your health. Be positive and work on yourself with katsugen and other suitable methods. To constantly work at bettering your health is your responsibility.

Mythical, moral, mysterious...
Let's open our inside shutters.
Who am I?
Who are you?
The innermost mind mutters...

MIND AND SPIRIT

Katsugen exercise is a method of tuning the natural health maintaining system of the body, but we must not forget that human beings are not merely a complex machine, but an amalgam of matter/energy, thought/mind, and soul/spirit. In achieving a well-balanced state of being, unifying as one the body, mind, and soul, there are self-maintenance methods that complement each other. Each person must choose the techniques that are best suited for him or herself that will enable the optimum of self-healing, self-realization and self-transcendence.

For me, katsugen exercise is what I use for physical self-maintenance; self-healing. It brings out the natural healing power within me that has been dulled and covered up by the dictates of society. How can I do this with my spirit? Like my body's urges, my spiritual leadings are often covered up by society's commands. How do I release the wellspring of positiveness that resides within?

In practicing katsugen, the mind steps aside and allows the body to move freely. In using katsugen to initiate spiritual movement, we similarly allow our minds to step aside and give assent to the soul to move toward the spirit.

We must dig deep, beyond the outward layers of memory and ego and into our very soul, and allow it to lead us even further inward to our spirit. Our spirit is the source of all that is positive. This is the root and foundation of all that we are. Once we tap into this source, anything is possible.

Pick a spot in your home where you can sit peacefully without being disturbed or interrupted. The key to becoming one with our spirit is to relax, but not too relaxed to the point of going to sleep. Abandon all fear, shame, remorse, guilt, hate, and feeling of lack. Realize that within you reside a part of the divine. A fragment of the Creator of the universe is at your center and guides you in all things. This is your spirit, the source of pure, unadulterated love. Feel this love and know that you are one with all the creatures in the entire universe.

Words cannot fully describe this oneness. It is beyond description because it is something that must be experienced to be truly understood. For now, it is enough to know that this state is worth attaining. Know that it is attainable and work towards it. I have included a few exercises at the end of this chapter. There are also many books on this subject. It is a transcendent feeling and is the greatest pleasure in the universe (see the chapter on pleasure). If you think you have achieved it and it is not the greatest pleasure, then it is not this state that I am speaking of.

Some call this state worshipful meditation, some say it is spiritual communion or the stillness. What it is called is not important. Getting into that state regularly is vital to optimum well-being.

Once we are able to attain this state of oneness on a regular basis, we can begin to undo society's attempts at blocking our spiritual leadings and start to bring out the positiveness that is inherent in the divine spark within.

Bringing Out The Positivity

Our minds are so conditioned by society. Why allow society to program and condition our minds with negativity, when we can fill ourselves with positivity? One of the simplest techniques for reinstating positivity is through affirmations. This is a method of self-programming one's bio-computer, our brain. Affirmations come in many shapes and forms. Repeating a mantra over and over again is a form of affirmation. A mantra is a phrase that has positive meaning such as, for example, "I reside in harmony with the universe." Many Eastern religions use mantras to reinforce their beliefs. Although simple, mantras are very powerful if practiced every day for long durations. I have chanted mantras for hours on end during one period of my life. Through chanting I even kicked a cold that was starting to come on.

Another form of affirmations is written on cards and repeated at set times such as in the morning and before bedtime. These affirmations are usually more specific than mantras. Some examples are, "I exude confidence in all that I do." "I am a brilliant spiritual being." "I finish what I start."

These affirmations are effective in correcting what you see in yourself as character flaws, vices, or negative tendencies.

It is important to remember when creating your own affirmations that they must come from your soul. You must truly identify with them and work towards that end. They are not "magic wish lists" that are intoned in hopes of something miraculous happening. Effort in its application is necessary.

They must also be positive. Rather than write, "I will not smoke." It is better to write, "I live a healthy lifestyle." Rather than, "I do not overeat." Write, "I eat healthily and in moderation." It is difficult to get excited over something not to do. That is because "to not do" something is to take something away. Affirmations are the most effective when they reinforce positive actions that we add to our lives.

The affirmations I mentioned above work to a certain extent but are not essentially of katsugen. There is a katsugen way of affirmations. Allow me to explain.

The katsugen induction exercises work by making the body exert itself in a way that is not intrinsically normal. In other words, when people normally exert their strength (for instance, imagine picking up something heavy) they clench their fist, project their ki forward and breathe in. The induction exercise does the abnormal thing: the fist is clenched with the thumb inside, the ki is projected to the rear and strength is exerted while breathing out. This throws the bodily system out of balance for a minute, which gets the autonomic nervous system working to get things under control. By becoming aware of the subtle effects of this balancing act, katsugen is initiated.

This is making use the law of physics that state that to every action, there is a reaction. To jump up, we bend our knees and shift our weight down first. To take a deep breath, we first breathe out. To send an arrow flying outward, we must first pull the string inward.

In using this method for affirmations, think first of the things about yourself that you dislike. Think about why you dislike those aspects of yourself. Don't make any excuses about them, just let them stay in your awareness for a while. Then, allow the natural positiveness inside you to assert your true self-value. Let your thoughts spring into where you're going – the desires you have, the dreams you are working towards, your aspirations, let it all come out like fireworks. Fill your thoughts with affirmations of making all those things come true. Stay in that space until you are satisfied. Go into spiritual communion if you desire.

The difference between the two kinds of affirmations is like night and day; like regular physical exercise and katsugen exercise. One is set and predetermined; the other is spontaneous and free. They are both necessary in order to achieve a balance.

These affirmations are useful techniques for the mind, but they work best if practiced in conjunction with the complementary techniques of the body and spirit – katsugen and worshipful meditation, on a regular basis. I usually do my affirmations and meditations twice a day: in the morning and at night, and I do katsugen once a day before going to bed. How you schedule these practices is entirely up to you based on the insights you receive from your "inner work."

Exercises for Stillness, Worshipful Meditation and Spiritual Communion

Both of the following are based on the katsugen philosophy of using action to get reaction. They both involve contemplating the tangible in order to find the intangible.

These deep meditational states take practice. If you have no experience in such things don't expect amazing results right away. (Transcendent results may occur immediately but they are the exception and not the rule.) Regularity and persistence is key. Designate a place in your home for this activity. Some people hang an inspirational picture on a wall and sit in front of it, using it to focus their mind. I have a small Buddhist altar, a remnant of the time I spent in Buddhist practice. Feel free to be creative or to use traditional methods, do what makes you comfortable.

Begin with just a few minutes every day, getting into the habit of sitting down and devoting a hundred percent of your being to accomplishing this. Remember, this is a pleasurable experience. Come away from each session with something positive, even if it is just the appreciation of having time to spend relaxed, unhurried, and devoted to self-improvement. Think of your personal spiritual growth as of the utmost priority, because it is. Realize that the rest of your day is based on these moments of inner work.

The following exercises do not have to be done exactly as is written. Use them as reference so that you can create what works best for you.

Converting Mind Chatter

One of the greatest obstacles to being mentally still is mind chatter. Thoughts come unbidden, seemingly out of nowhere. Try to think of nothing and everything fills the mind.

It is possible to convert this noisy energy into peace and tranquility.

Instead of fighting this flow of thought, relax into it. Go more deeply into each and every thought that appears. Inspect and analyze every little sound that you hear, every irritating itch on your skin, and every reminder of your past. Delve fully into each and every chattering thought until you are mentally exhausted. Then, suddenly, think, what is left? Take away all of those conscious thoughts and see into the core of your mind. Look beyond into the space behind the mind chatter and what will you find?

If you have found even a split second of nothingness, you will have found a basis for the stillness. For in nothingness, there is everything. Practice going to this space everyday until you can transport yourself there at will.

Exploring the Universe/The One and the Whole

Use your imagination and think of your spirit inside your body. Think of your body in the room you are in. Think of your body in the room in the house. Think of your body in the room in the house in the neighborhood. Think of your body in the room in the house in the neighborhood in your part of the city or town. Continue with this and increase the scale by increments: the city to the county, the county to the state, the state to the country, the country to the continent, the continent to the planet, the planet to the solar system, the solar system to the galactic spiral arm and on and on until you come to the entire universe as you know it.

Identify with the whole universe. Imagine the countless beings all connected together through the Universe Source. Imagine the waves crashing on countless shores. Winds whistling through a billion forests, love flowing through a multitude of hearts. Know that you are one with them. That the universe is friendly. Be at peace with everything. Become everything and you can become as nothing – still and in harmony with all.

The wavy, navy ocean beckons,
her stinging salt spray soothes.
I long to unleash my body
in her crystal cool blue.

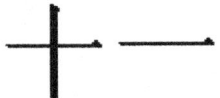

PLEASURE

Pleasure is not an option. Pleasure is a requirement for a happy, fulfilling life. I am speaking not only of the pleasures of the physical senses but also of the profound pleasures of achieving a goal, of personal relationships, of being of service to others, of creating a work of art, of raising children and the myriad of activities and pursuits which yield bounties of fulfillment, satisfaction, reward and achievement.

The less capacity for pleasure we have, the more humdrum and meaningless our existence.

Many of the pleasures associated with the physical senses have to do with relief. The pleasure of eating is a relief from the pressure of hunger. The pleasure of sex is a relief from the pressure of our reproductive needs. Entertainment is relief from the pressure of work. Exercise is relief from the pressure of inactivity. In a sense, these pleasures are "negative", not in a bad way but in that they result from doing away the pressure; they are subtractive, not additive.

There are "higher" pleasures. Pleasures that result not from relief but from adding positive energy. Those activities I mentioned above: creative works, personal relationships, raising children, etc., are "positive". They add rich new experiences to our souls that are indeed pleasurable, not in an immediate, sensational way as are the pleasures of the senses, but on a longer lasting, more profound level. Spiritual communion and worshipful meditation, on this deeper level, has been said to be the most pleasurable experience in the universe. Personally, I have found this to be true. However, this not the sensual pleasure of the flesh, but rather of the soul. It is peace and wholeness that transcends the wants of the physical body.

Generally, we begin to desire more of these "positive" pleasures as we grow older, but yet, we must still be in contact with the child within us, the child that seeks tactile pleasures in the world around us. For these pleasures of the senses keep us grounded and in touch with the world of nature, of material reality. Again, balance is necessary, balance between the pleasures of the mind and soul and the pleasures of the senses.

The things that used to give us pleasure when we were young lose its gloss as we age. We begin to look for pleasure in things that have more intricacy and meaning, and become jaded to the simple things that used to hold so much sway in our hearts. We lose the eyes of children. We cease to see as children.

When we put so much time and effort into our work at the expense of seeing the pleasures of everyday life and the simple beauties of nature, we have indeed lost something. As I stated in my previous chapter, work can be fun and enjoyable, but the more we take it seriously, and the more pressure we put on ourselves to work harder, the less fun it can become. So we take a vacation. Have some fun to break up the tedium of everyday work. Again, balance.

Katsugen can revive our capacity for pleasure. Katsugen is the micro-vacation we can indulge in on a daily basis. It unshackles us from the controlling thoughts that keep us from having fun. How many ways of having fun do you know? And how many reasons for not doing them can you think of?

Delaying gratification is one of the hallmarks of maturity. When we were young, immediate gratification was the rule. As we grew wiser, we began to realize that immediate pleasures must be put off in order to reap them later on after the job has been done. Then we venture into the other extreme, of delaying gratification for so long we lose taste for it. Fasting for too long of a duration is a health risk, because after a period of time, the body loses all desire for food. When we continue upon a course of action for too long, inertia takes over and it becomes hard to break the trend. The same with putting off pleasure. How often do we hear of workaholics being ordered by their doctors to take some time off?

Practicing katsugen regularly keeps us in balance. We manifest the child in our bodies, allowing it to come forth in simplicity, always in awe and wonder at the cosmos, willing to play, to relax, to have fun, to revel in the joys of being a child of the universe.

When I'm without
I feel so worn out.
Time feels like a spider web
with me the spider.
Waiting for something juicy.

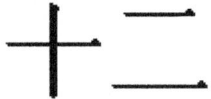

DRUGS

Prescription drugs, caffeine, nicotine, alcohol, marijuana, aspirin, cocaine, heroin, antihistamines, amphetamines, antibiotics and on and on, our world is inundated with drugs. They are all medicine, and like anything else, they are used and abused.

Prescriptions are given to us by doctors. "Over-the-counter" drugs, socially accepted drugs (caffeine, alcohol, nicotine) and illegal recreational drugs are self-administered. The self-administered drugs are the ones that give us the most problems, not to say that prescription drugs are problem free.

Katsugen is a great barometer for the effects of drugs on the body. I had experimented with some drugs in my youth and found that because I practiced katsugen, my body reacted very strongly to them. Because of this sensitivity, I was able to control usage and was able to keep from being irretrievably harmed.

Drugs are medicine, and while all things should be done in moderation, drugs are especially pertinent to this admonition. It is often the things that give the most pleasure that has the most potential for dangerous abuse: sex, eating, and drugs being three popular examples. (Even the pleasure of worshipful communion can lead to abuse - fanaticism.) "Miracle" drugs such as antibiotics, once thought to be a cure-all for all bacterial infections are nowadays often overused and abused. Because of the overuse of antibiotics, we are in danger of creating antibiotic resistant germs, "superbugs" that cannot be killed by ordinary antibiotics. Over-reliance on medicine is dangerous. The best way to health is to strengthen our immune system and other self-defense mechanisms of the body.

The autonomic nervous system is what the body uses to coordinate the cells, tissues and organs. When we ingest mind and function altering substances, many parts of the body are utilized in ways that are not according to the usual "plan". For instance, caffeine stimulates the heart and respiratory system, increases muscular tremor, and produces more stomach acid throwing the system off balance and making the autonomic nervous system work overtime. If we pay close attention to our body and how the autonomic nervous system is functioning, we can stop abuse before damage is done. Through katsugen, we can curb our tendencies to overindulge before serious trouble impairs our health by keeping in touch with our autonomic nervous system, actualized by the process of organic bio-feedback through movement.

This also works with "natural" drugs. By natural drugs, I don't mean herbs and organic medicine, but rather the substances in our bodies like hormones and neurochemicals such as endorphins, dopamine, testosterone, serotonin, oxytocin, etc. that affect our state of being. It is becoming more and more clear through scientific discoveries that our state of consciousness and well-being is directly influenced in ways that are very profound by these internal drugs. And contrary to what some may say, I believe these natural drugs are just as addictive and can be just as detrimental to our peace of mind and productivity as any artificial drug. Man-made drugs are clearly visible in society and we can consciously make a detour around them. But internal drugs are invisible and so much a part of us that they are triggered subconsciously by circumstances, and it is only through self-mastery that we can control their effects on us. Katsugen can help attain this mastery.

The body is a coat for the mind,
the mind is a shirt for the soul.
Scrub your soul a layer at a time,
and be naked with the spirit you find.

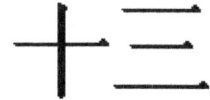

APPEARANCE

Will katsugen help you lose weight and make you look good?

I believe it can, in many cases, but I am not a medical scientist and I have no data to prove it. Weight control is a complex subject that is affected by environment, heredity, diet and culture. It depends on each particular case but even when the regular practice of katsugen moves you toward an ideal weight, it is not an "instant fix."

Logically, being slim and staying slim would seem to require only one thing: to expend as much energy as you take in. To lose weight, one only needs to put out more energy than you put in. It seems so simple, but of course, it is not.

Biologically, we're made so that it's easier to keep our energy in the form of fat than to use it in the form of exercise. Why? It used to be extremely difficult to find food; humans lived for millions of years with not enough to eat; and hunting, gathering and growing food took up much of the food's energy that we did manage to procure. So what we did find and eat, our bodies were very efficient at keeping as stored energy - fat. It was a matter of survival.

In much of our past history, being fat was looked upon as a sign of wealth and prosperity. Currently, the view of corpulency is much more negative. We know now that it is even a health hazard.

We're living in a civilization where we have more than enough to eat, but our bodies do not realize that, it still wants to hoard that energy as if our survival depended on it. How do we convince our bodies that it's okay to use up the stored fat energy?

First of all, our bodies must want to eat the right foods: currently, common nutritional wisdom recommends complex carbohydrates, fruits and vegetables, protein and some fat. Secondly, our bodies must exercise or somehow use the energy we take in.

Once you have a good feedback loop with your body through katsugen, you will know immediately the effects of eating the right foods or the wrong foods. You will also know when you need to exercise. You will begin to *desire* eating good quality food and to exercise. Many people who are naturally in tune with their autonomic nervous system have this without katsugen, but they also quite often lose it over time or by overindulging in one thing or another. Regular practice of katsugen keeps you on top of it.

One of the reasons I believe that some people eat too much or eat too much junk food is because eating is the main pleasure in life for them. They "live to eat" rather "eat to live" to paraphrase Ben Franklin. By developing more wholesome pleasures in life, the focus on eating for fun can be diminished while at the same time those added pastimes can help you use up more energy. As I mentioned in the chapter on pleasures, katsugen can restore the child within you so that your capacity for creative pleasure is increased. Become varied in the interests you have in life, have less fun eating and more fun in ways that expend energy rather than in intaking it.

There are limits, though, to what any diet, exercise regimen and even surgery can do. We are stuck with certain physical traits that cannot be changed. Our height, our bone structure, certain medical conditions, and body types are "hands" that we are dealt with. However, we can always make the best of it. Even the worst "hand" can be a winning "hand" if played by a resourceful and positive mind and soul.

What is truly important is how healthy you are and how good you feel. Body styles are often determined by culture. Plump ladies were once the vogue and they still are in some parts of the world. In our society, models that look like waifs are "in" right now, but who knows how long it will last?

Most of us will never be among the so-called "beautiful" people. But we are, all of us, truly beautiful. There most definitely is an inner beauty that transcends outer physical beauty, which we can access with katsugen. This beauty is not "skin deep" nor is it dictated by the passing trends of time, age and culture. It is the beauty of balance, of integration of body, mind and soul and its manifestation as loving action and service to others. This beauty brings us both inner joy and outer satisfaction. It is not made up of one facet of our selves but it is a coordinated amalgam that brings the best out of our imperfections to create something new, original and unique. It is beauty in the truest sense of the word.

We must remember, though, that this inner beauty is unlike physical attractiveness. It does not turn heads, but it will turn souls. It will not bring you one night stands, but long lasting relationships. You will not have countless lovers for it but rather the one precious soul mate that lasts into the mists of time.

This beauty is not necessarily easy to live in, for it must be nurtured daily, cultivated and vitalized. Sometimes it will even be lonely when surrounded by a society that knows only the beauty of the flesh, but it is more real than anything and when one comes to that realization, the whole universe will radiate peace and goodwill, and physical appearance becomes merely a shadow cast by the light of true reality and total being-ness.

It is here now, tap into it!

Men try to be immovable,
women irresistible,
it's all because of our egos.
But fortunately, neither succeeds
because we are all too damn flexible.

十四

TIME AND FAITH

"Time heals all wounds", so it is said, and given enough time, it is literally true. Time is one of the most vital elements to healing and is often the most neglected to our detriment. People are so impatient to get well that they do not realize that the body needs time in order to right itself. Case in point: antibiotics are over-prescribed by physicians because patients who come down with a relatively minor infection desire to get over it as quickly as possible. They say they do not have the time to wait for the body's immune system to kick in. Unfortunately, this is counterproductive in the long run because frequent usage of antibiotics prevents the body from maintaining a healthy and strong immune system. Plus, when antibiotic resistant bacterial arise, antibiotics become useless and with a weakened immune system the body is helpless to combat bacterial infection.

There is a tendency among some of us to worry when we come down with pain, discomfort, nausea and other symptoms for which we do not know the reason, especially when it persists over a period of time. In many cases, these symptoms will disappear in a few days; they are merely passing conditions for which the body adjusts in due course with its self-righting mechanisms, especially when we put into practice katsugen and/or other self-healing methods. When the symptoms worsen or persist, we may go see a physician or alternative medical practitioner. When all the above has been done, and the problem still continues, time and patience may be the answer. Relax, and take stock of yourself. Allow the medication, the treatment or the healing technique to work. Meanwhile, have faith that you are healing and that all is well.

Who are you?

You are defined
by your relationship
with your environment;
by what you value.

So, in essence,
you are what you value.

十五

SELF-MASTERY

To be able to control oneself is something that one takes for granted. As adults we have control of ourselves most of the time, or do we? Looking at the problems we have such as obesity, substance abuse, anger, hate, intolerance, violence and self-actualized illnesses, we can see that this is an area of self-development that still needs a lot of work.

The main reason self-mastery is so difficult for some people is because they are thinking about it in the wrong way. The error in thinking is that they treat parts of themselves as enemies to conquer and destroy through sheer force of will. They split themselves into two: there is the "you" that does the undesirable things, like eating or drinking too much, getting angry, not doing enough, doing too much, etc. then there is the "you" that is critical of the other "you" and has all kinds of suggestions as to how to correct yourself. So, in effect, you are fighting against yourself. And your life becomes a constant battle between the two opposing sides of your mind, in a sense, the angel and the devil sitting on your shoulder. Sometimes the angel wins the battle, sometimes the devil wins. But the war continues on and on. No one wins for good because there is no unity, no cohesiveness, and no wholeness. A divided personality is a fragmented personality; it is indecision personified. Self-mastery over the long term must be based on making decisions as a whole person.

It is time to end the war. To quit fighting yourself. Think of your habits and vices, not as enemies but as friends, after all they are parts of yourself. Be okay with yourself as you are. Be whole, present and in the moment all the time - mindful. When you take a bite from that cheesecake, be a hundred percent present and aware of what you are doing. Enjoy it. Savor it. Still the nagging and critical mind. Think about where the food came from, where it's going, how your body will utilize it. Appreciate it.

It is important to be mindful because when certain behavior becomes habit, it means that you are not doing it volitionally; it has been put on autopilot and it will keep on repeating itself automatically.

Things you do that affect your health should be done with 100% volition and wholeness of intent. Make it a practice to act from the whole of yourself. Even when you act on your undesirable habit, enjoy it and do it with no conflict within you, no guilt, shame or holding back, do it as a person making a decision as a whole – body, mind and soul. Then when you want to quit, you are able to do it as a whole being, with no conflict within.

However, to be 100% whole means there has to be implementation, coordination and direction for your body, mind and soul. The soul directs, the mind coordinates and the body implements your decisions.

The importance of the soul directing is that self-mastery is dependent on our values, and the soul is the repository of our spiritual values. Whether we decide to act in one way or another, to live healthily or not, to do good things or not, depends on our values. So let your soul make the decisions, for that is the best part of you. If you give your body the power to call the shots, you will indulge in everything the body wants – an animalistic life. If you give your mind the power to rule your life, you will do things that are based only on your intellect – a logical but cold and robotic life. Give the soul authority to choose your path and your life will be well balanced and whole.

However, it is not easy for most people to allow the soul to make decisions. For what is the soul to them? How can they differentiate the urgings of the body from the whisperings of the mind and the leadings of the soul?

By paying attention to your inner energies you can become more aware of the forces that are in play within yourself, and learn to channel these energies creatively and productively for health and happiness. Through katsugen, one can get a good feel of these inner dynamics. Once one achieves a working understanding of the body, mind, soul and spirit, one can use meditation to actualize the true self. To attain self-mastery you have to first determine who the self is, who you truly are, and that is up to you to decide.

I walk toward the distant light
with my heart in my hands,
my spirit beckons to my soul
yearning for better lands.

AFTERWORD

Katsugen exercise is wonderful and physically liberating. The exercise has enabled me to formulate katsugen, the philosophy, which has been such a boon to my life that I had to share it by writing this book.

Words, actually, are insufficient to describe katsugen exercise. Seeing somebody else do the exercise helps, but even that is not always enough for someone to "get it". In a way, it is like the air. You can't grasp it with your hand but it is all around you. The way to understand katsugen exercise is to not try so hard at figuring out what it is. Just do the induction movements and let it flow of its own accord. Some of you may take to it right away, while others may require a longer time. It is even possible that you will give up for a long while, only to come back to it in the future when your body requires it.

This book is a result of my experiences that came from a practice taught me by Noguchi-san. Presently, as far as I know, there are no medical data or documentation that support claims that katsugen exercise is beneficial to one's health. It is my hope that, eventually, enough people will practice this exercise so that medical science will get curious enough to perform some clinical tests regarding its efficacy in health maintenance.

Regarding katsugen, the philosophy, it is something that cannot be analyzed by scientific tests. However much of the wisdom and ideas of this philosophy are rooted in the ancient healing practices of Buddhism, Taoism and other Eastern disciplines and is time tested. The proof of its value will be in the lives of those who live it and the acts they perform in service to the world.

Printed in Great Britain
by Amazon